Grey Hair
& You

Grey Hair and You

Copyright © Penelope Jane Whiteley 2017 All Rights Reserved
The rights of Penelope Jane Whiteley to be identified as the author of this work have been asserted in accordance with the Copyright, Designs and Patents Act 1988
All rights reserved. No part may be reproduced, adapted, stored in a retrieval system or transmitted by any means, electronic, mechanical, photocopying, or otherwise without the prior written permission of the author or publisher.

Spiderwize
Remus House
Coltsfoot Drive
Woodston
Peterborough
PE2 9BF

www.spiderwize.com

A CIP catalogue record for this book is available from the British Library.

Requests for permission or more information should be sent to pjw@penelopewhiteley.com

Some information sources are printed at the back of the book

This book/ebook are designed to provide information regarding the topic and subject matter covered. Any application of the recommendations set forth in this book/ebook are at the reader's discretion and sole risk.

While all attempts have been made to verify information provided in this publication, neither the author nor the publisher assumes any responsibility for errors, omissions or contrary interpretation on the subject matter.

The purchaser or reader of this publication assumes full responsibility for the use of these materials and information. Adherence to all applicable laws and regulations, in relevant jurisdiction is the sole responsibility of the purchaser or reader. The author and publisher assume no responsibility or liability whatsoever on the behalf of any purchaser or reader of these materials. The purpose of this book/ebook is to educate, inform, and entertain.

ISBN: 978-1-911596-29-5

Grey Hair & You

PENELOPE JANE WHITELEY

Preface

This is not the tale of a cathartic journey on the joys, or not, of acquiring grey hair. It is, quite simply, advice on what to do with your grey hair when you've got it. It is the result of all the questions asked by the women over 50 who I have worked with over the years. As a coach and mentor, I find it fascinating that the greatest problem women over 50 seem to face is their grey hair.

So here it is, warts 'n all. The book that takes you from why hair turns grey to the right way to bleach grey hair, tips for taming wiry grey hair and even make-up tips for looking great with grey hair. If you have questions, you will find the answers here ... including what to do with your eyebrows! It contains the answers to almost every question asked about hair by women of a certain age; all packaged in one little book

You will find images throughout the book, which don't necessarily relate to the chapter or section in which they're included. This is because it's almost impossible to find images that actually work with the text; although I suppose I could have made a habit of haunting hairdressing salons on the off-chance ...

There are images of various ladies, all looking gorgeous, all grey haired or salt-and-pepper, and all doing something about it! There are also images of me over a 20 year period, which clearly show the transition from dark hair (before there was any grey), to highlights and lowlights.

Gratitude and thanks to my friends who have helped along the way (you know who you are); and I owe a special debt of gratitude to Zaharoula Harris of Zed Photography, whose images are featured throughout the book.

I hope you enjoy this little offering and find the information useful.

Introduction

Women often have mixed emotions about their hair turning grey. Whatever colour they were when they were younger, whether they were a brunette, a blonde or a redhead, is inextricably linked to their identity.

When you think of grey hair, you think of your grandparents, your parents, and the folks down in the Old People's Home. You certainly don't think of yourself!

Of course, for those women who can hardly remember what their natural hair colour is (they've been dyeing it for so many years), finding their roots are now more grey than coloured, can be even more distressing.

Why is greying hair such a problem for women? Because for us all, the first grey hair is a sign of the inexorable approach of old age. Most women feel a sense of loss when their hair begins to change ... when the gray hairs become more in number than their original colour.

There also seems to be a social stigma associated with grey hair which, in reality, is a social stigma towards aging. But it is society's attitude that needs to change towards grey hair and aging; not ours!

Nevertheless, grey hair causes worry and distress to us all, to a greater or lesser extent. Hence the reason for this book ... learn the best ways to colour grey hair, how to bleach it effectively, how to transition from coloured to grey, and make-up tips to transform your look. You will even learn how to colour **your grey eyebrows!**

If you're looking for a little more science, there are links at the back of the book to lead you to sites where you can get some scientific and medical information.

Contents

Preface 5

Introduction 7

I. Why Does Hair Turn Grey? 13
Grey Hair At The Cellular Level 13
Genetics & Myths About Grey Hair 14

II. Busting Myths About Grey Hair 19
Myth #1: Grey Hairs Multiply. 19
Myth #2: Fright Will Turn Your Hair Grey. 20
Not So Much A Myth #1: Stress Turns Your Hair Grey .. 21
Not So Much A Myth #2:
Smoking Makes You Grey Haired Younger 21

III. Five Colouring Tips For Greying Hair 23
The 5 Golden Rules For Colouring Grey Hair 24
1. Always, Always, Always Do a Colour Test First 24
2. Don't be Afraid to Move On 25
3. Take Advantage of Highlights 27
4. Not Everything Is Absolute
When It Comes To Grey Hair 29
5. Treat Yourself To The Occasional Salon Visit 30

IV. The Right Way To Bleach Grey Hair 32
Having A Plan To Go From
A Dyed Dark Colour to Grey 33
If You Are More Than 30% Grey 34
Bleaching Blonde To Grey 35

Fade To Grey Instead Of Bleaching To White 36

V. Making The Transition From Dyed To Grey Hair ... 38
Let's Start With What Is Possible.. 39
Cutting Your Hair 40
Streaking Your Hair Colour 41
The Courage to Transition 41
Planning Your Transition 42

VI. Tips for Taming Wiry Grey Hair 43
Removing The Frizz From Your Hair 43
Lessons In Using Hair Products 45
Weathering The Weather 46

VII. 7 Silver-Haired Foxes Whose Hair Styles You May Want To Copy 48
Jamie Lee Curtis. 49
Dame Judi Dench. 49
Helen Mirren. 50
Blythe Danner. 50
Meryl Streep. 51
Dianne Keaton. 51
Carmen Dell'Orefice. 52

VIII. Helping Your Grey Hair To Look Thicker And Fuller 54
Your Weapons For Thick, Full Looking Hair 54
Handling Fine Hair 56
What Your Hairdresser Does To Create Volume 57

IX. Make-up Tips For Looking Great With Grey Hair. 59

    Start With The Basics 59
    Adding A Fresh Glow 60
    Helping Lips Look Luscious 61
    Definition & Colour For Your Eyes 61

Getting New Ideas For Your Make-up 62

X. Tips For Colouring Grey Eyebrows 64
    Problems With Tinting Eyebrows 64
    Follow The Steps To Get It Right 65
    They Won't Change Colour! 67
    An Alternative 68

Finally 70

About Penelope Jane Whiteley 72

I. Why Does Hair Turn Grey?

The first grey hair, or the hundredth, causes us to ask the question : why does hair turn grey? Actually, what we really want is to learn how to prevent the grey from creeping in ... and it's unlikely we'll find an answer because in reality, there isn't one ... but knowing why hair turns grey, might at least make us all feel a little better.

Grey Hair At The Cellular Level

To get to the reason behind greying hair, you need to dig a little deeper than the hair itself. Hair doesn't come pre-coloured, so to speak; it is coloured by the pigment melanin, which is produced in the cells of your hair follicles. It's quite a complicated process in which melanocytes (pigment forming cells) inject melanin into the keratin hair shaft (Keratin is the protein that makes up our hair, nails and skin), and give your hair its colour. As you get older, the melanocytes slow and eventually stop injecting melanin into the hair shaft, and so the colour pigment stops being produced. The result is hair that looks grey.

The grey hair time-line is different for everyone. Some people get their first grey hair in their teens. Some don't get a strand until their late thirties, or even into their fifties. While it's a general rule that Caucasians become grey younger than people of Asian or African background, scientists believe that the age at which you turn grey has a lot to do with your individual genetic inheritance. In other words, coming from an Asian background is no guarantee of long-term glossy locks if grandma went grey at 16!

HAIR ANATOMY

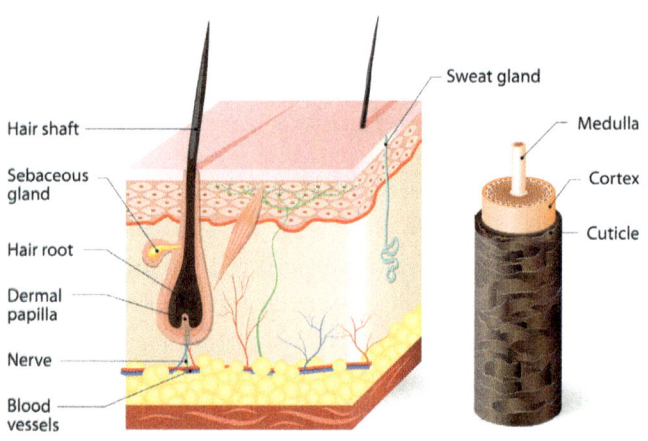

Genetics & Myths About Grey Hair

Is there any truth in the urban myth that a sudden shock can turn people grey overnight? Well yes and no; it can happen, but only over a period of time (weeks, months, and years); so no, not overnight!

But, if you have a rare disease called '*Diffuse Alopecia Areata*' (which is believed to be a hereditary condition), you hair can turn grey overnight.

As for grey hair being caused by stress, in one sense stress may have something to do with greying hair, but not in the way you're thinking. Your hair grows in cycles and each individual hair has its own cycle; it's on your head, it falls out and is replaced. We've known for a long time that grey hair is the result of the gradual decline in activity of melanin-producing follicle cells (melanocytes). But why do these cells stop working?

Scientists now believe that grey hair is a result of a build-up of hydrogen peroxide, which is produced naturally within the body, and which causes stress to the melanocytes, the cells that produce melanin; which is why we **can** say stress causes grey hair. In younger bodies, hydrogen peroxide is broken down by an enzyme called catalase. As we age, less of this enzyme is produced. Essentially, we become walking pre-mixed bottle blondes as the excess hydrogen peroxide affects the cells.

The decrease in the levels of catalase and the increase in the levels of hydrogen peroxide cannot be reversed. There is no magical cure; it is simply part of the aging process, although there are some scientists trying to find a solution by developing cosmetic treatments based on catalase.

This doesn't explain why some people start greying younger than others, and the fall-back answer is still 'genetics'. If your mother and your mother's mother became grey young, you guessed it - your youthful grey hair is inevitable.

According to a survey by hairtrade.com, British women will each spend up to £40,000 in their lifetime on cutting, colouring and styling at the hairdressers; more than the average house deposit.

In the USA, the average woman will spend up to $100 per month (the average is $48 to $85) to keep her hair dyed, which seems excessive. But the figure includes visits to hairdressers and it's important to work out what you're actually paying for at the hairdressers. Self-colouring, the colour-in-a-box, will never provide you with the result you get from a professional. You may know what you want, but you seldom get what you want. It's just the nature of the beast.

The diagram on the right shows the difference in the shape of a hair shaft shape for straight and curly blondes, straight and curly black/brown, and straight and curly grey; this is what happens to the shaft when your hair turns grey! As you can see, the shaft contains air pockets, which mysteriously appear in the hair shaft and contribute to the greying process by blocking the path of Melanin.

Basis of Hair Color and Texture

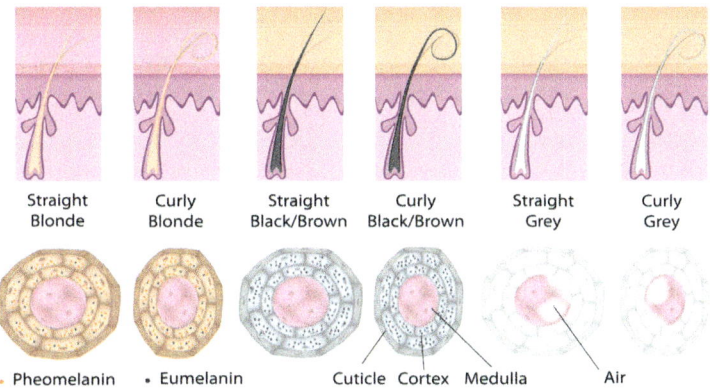

Although this may not be good timing for you, researchers at University College London have discovered the grey hair gene.

The discovery of the gene responsible for greying hair, IRF4, means that in the future changing hair (or even eye colour!) may be possible without using dyes. Simply by taking a drug to alter appearance, blondes could become brunettes and grey hair could be prevented. But don't rush off to your doctor for the magic potion just yet; the research has only just begun!

As a side note, the lack of pigment that results in your grey hair also makes your hair more brittle, because your hair loses its elasticity, and the cuticle, that protects each strand, becomes thinner . Which means when the grey comes in, it's time to start looking after your hair with a little more tenderness. You need to identify a shampoo, and a really nourishing conditioner, that are kind to your greying hair now that it is more fragile.

In the future it may be possible to prevent hair greying and not impossible to reverse grey hair. This may sound like a miracle and worries hairdressers, but always remember, grey hair is nature's way of softening the appearance of our faces as we age.

II. Busting Myths About Grey Hair

Greying hair is often regarded with horror because it may be one of the first physical signs of aging.

We all look for reasons we have it, and hope vainly that we can find some way to slow its growth or put a hold on the grey hair altogether. Unfortunately, some of the longest-lived urban myths do nothing to help us accept those little strands of silver populating our locks, and it's time some of them were banished ...

Myth #1: Grey Hairs Multiply.

One of the myths about hair plucking, shaving and trimming is that a plucked grey hair will result in the growth of five more, or many more, depending on which version of the myth you have heard.

This is, quite simply, rubbish! Head hairs grow individually, and follicles will not gang up on you when you rip them out in order to sprout some sort of crazy-hair-growth-vengeance upon you. This is not a horror movie; although it may feel like one.

Scientists in white coats probably find it very amusing when they hear some of the things we non-scientists can be tricked into believing.

Myth #2: Fright Will Turn Your Hair Grey.

People seem to attribute hair follicles with great emotional range; I'm not sure why. Apparently not only are they offended when a fellow hair is plucked, but they somehow sense when a ghost is nearby or react violently to a traumatic or shocking event!

This myth is as big a piece of rubbish as **grey hairs multiply**. While extreme stress can result in some temporary hair loss, no-one has ever had their hair spontaneously turn grey from fright; hair turns grey over weeks, months and years; it just feels as though it's overnight

There **is** a particular genetic trait **plus** a very specific disease, called *Alopecia Areata*, that has been claimed to turn hair grey overnight. But you must have the two in exactly the right combination at the same time.

Scientific evidence has yet to verify that fright or shock is the trigger for the onset of hair spontaneously changing from colour to grey.

As we all know though, some old wives' tales have a grain of truth in them. For every grey hair myth that is unequivocally untrue, there is another that isn't completely off the mark.

Not So Much A Myth #1: Stress Turns Your Hair Grey

While we all probably need to slow down a little, there's now another reason to de-stress; your hair.

A link between the hydrogen peroxide our bodies naturally produce and greying hair has revealed a very small grain of truth in this myth.

Our bodies produce more hydrogen peroxide when we're stressed; and hydrogen peroxide affects the melanin-producing cells (melanocytes) in hair follicles. The suggestion is that less stress means less hydrogen peroxide and therefore little to no grey hair caused by stress.

That makes yoga or meditation, combined with an anti-oxidant diet, an excellent remedy for de-stressing and a way to slow down the grey.

Not So Much A Myth #2: Smoking Makes You Grey Haired Younger

Yes. Apparently grey hair progresses at an increased rate if you are a smoker.

Various studies have shown that smokers are two and a half times more likely to go grey prematurely (under the age of 30); some research shows a four times increase in premature grey hair.

Whichever is right, and as with everything, there is an argument "for and against" this myth, we can also say smoking has been linked to premature graying and loss of hair, although the supporting evidence remains circumstantial.

Doctors from University Hospital in Zurich, Switzerland found that cigarette smoke may damage the DNA in hair follicles as well as constrict blood vessels that supply the follicles. That means thinner hair and more hair loss. The answer? Don't smoke!

In reality though, going grey is just another part of the aging process ... the age at which you will get your first grey hair is largely determined by genetics, but the rate at which the greying progresses is largely under your own control.

Besides smoking, other factors that can speed up the greying process are anaemia, poor nutrition, insufficient B vitamins (stress again), and untreated thyroid conditions.

Good nutrition is always the same! A poor diet can induce oxidative stress which is linked to premature gray hair; and so is a low level of Vitamin B12. Stress again.

Looking after your health has long been thought to slow down the greying process. Eating well, exercising more and smoking less may not permanently keep greys away, but they're good ideas nonetheless; and not just for your hair.

III. Five Colouring Tips For Greying Hair

*"Look at Helen Mirren. Isn't she gorgeous?
She's gorgeous, and she even has grey hair!
How does she do it?"*

Obviously, not everyone has the resources of an Oscar-winning Hollywood actress when it comes to dealing with grey hair, but there are plenty of things anyone can do to make their grey hair look fabulous. Whether you're looking to highlight the silver, or tone it down, the most important thing is to be a little more considerate of the condition of your hair.

Before:
Salt and pepper

After
PHOTO COURTESY OF
ZED PHOTOGRAPHY

The 5 Golden Rules For Colouring Grey Hair

1. Always, Always, Always Do a Colour Test First

ALWAYS! This rule cannot be emphasised enough.

Grey hair can react unpredictably to colour and because different people have different shades of grey, **you can't take it for granted that a colour that works for your best friend will give you the same result**. Even when you're using special grey hair colour, preferably without Ammonia.

It's worth taking the extra time to test. Trust me, having hot pink hair instead of luscious brown can be a bit of a shock for anyone... and you don't want to be trying something like this for the first time on the same day you're supposed to be going out to a glamorous soirée. I know; because I once did just that!

Colour **test your chosen colour on a discreet area of your hair**. The back, or an area hidden under other locks, is a good idea. You might need a mirror and hair clips to help you if you're doing the test on your own. If you have long hair, it can be easier to simply snip off a lock for the test.

Remember that **hair colour companies occasionally change their formulas**, so it's a good idea to test every time, even though it can be a real pain and is definitely a chore.

Of course, if you're the adventurous type and happy to proudly wear whatever colour hair you end up with ... go for it ...

2. Don't be Afraid to Move On

We all get attached to our existing colour, but it's important to remember as our hair greys, your skin tones change as well. Dyeing to your original hair colour becomes obviously fake when your complexion tone changes and you become pale, or sallow. Besides, a solid line of dark colour (possibly your original hair colour) is too harsh as you start to age and can add years to your appearance. No hair is ever one solid colour, and we turn grey because the universe is being kind to us and providing us with a softness around our faces.

You'll notice that the most attractive older women in the public eye are those who have greyed gracefully over time; or allowed their original colour to continuously fade a little over a long period of time, until they have a perfectly balanced blend of colour and grey. Or they have become blonde!

The honest truth, as hard as it can be to hear, is that **strong or bright hair colours just don't go well with older skin tones**. Something that Hollywood and every other stylist knows; they ensure their A-list clients, as well as their non-famous clients, are never caught out by this issue.

Stick with a helmet-head of full-coloured hair at your peril!

Unless you choose to be daring and different; choosing spikey, purple hair is just that. Not for the faint-hearted, this type of look is usually paired with a lot of panache and belongs to a woman without fear ...

Gossip magazines and some newspapers, but especially social media, are ruthlessly truthful and let celebrities know they look awful, when they persist with strong hair colour long after they should have changed to a colour more suitable to their complexion; everyone lets them know, in no uncertain terms.

For us mere mortals, people close to us will be ultra-considerate of our feelings to the point of lying (!), and your hairdresser isn't going to say anything for fear of losing you as a client.

Your best option is to do what the stylists do for top celebrities like Helen Mirren and Jane Fonda, and gradually **transition to a new hair colour** by slowly introducing a slightly gentler shade of your original hair colour, and allow a few more grey/silver/white streaks to show through each time.

When you chose to transition by colouring your hair differently, over time you'll discover that you've achieved a beautiful mane of colour blended with grey that looks striking, fits perfectly with your complexion and makes you look radiant, just like the stylish elite. If that's what you want ...

This image of a friend of mine is a classic example of what happens when you're not looking. After years of colouring her hair blonde, she suddenly realised her roots were lighter than the colour she was applying. This is the natural result of abandoning the colouring process ... fabulous ...

3. Take Advantage of Highlights

Speaking of highlights (or lowlights, or foils, or whatever you call them), they are your grey hair's best friend.

Any **hair colour looks better, and more natural, when there is a variation of tone**. This is because hair naturally takes on different tones in different places; mainly because of exposure to the elements, but also just because our body chemistry is so complex, and it seems the universe likes a bit of chaos.

When colouring at home, buy and use a hair colour that incorporates highlights. If you don't have access to these types of hair colouring products in your area, consider using two slightly different hair colours. Put one colour through and when it's dry, comb the second, lighter colour through your hair to achieve a blended, high-lighting effect.

When you first become aware that your hair colour is no longer working with your skin tone, it's worth consulting **a professional hairdresser** who has a reputation for making mature women look fantastic. Check out glamour magazines, and in the back section of listings, find the details of the hairdresser near you that fits the bill, or find them online.

A single extravagantly expensive appointment with such a hairdresser can be very helpful in finding a style that you can then get your regular hairdresser to replicate, at a fraction of the cost.

Once your expensive appointment is over, and you're thrilled with the result, take a photograph of your hair from lots of different vantage points, so you can show the pictures to your regular hairdresser. It's basically like taking in a magazine picture of a hair style you want; only it's personalised.

If cost is a consideration, why not try a hairdressing school? Once you know exactly what you want and they can see the result, they do an amazing job for a fraction of the price. They are eager to please and there is always a professional on hand; they don't do anything to your hair until their tutor has discussed the treatment with them at length.

4. *Not Everything Is Absolute When It Comes To Grey Hair*

We talk about 'grey', 'silver' and 'white' hair but actually there are so many shades that it's impossible to classify them all.

Add to that the skin tone variations of each individual and **you've got a totally unique colour combination that is specific to you**. Sisters and even twins can have very different colouring issues when it comes to grey hair.

The dilemma is that, whether we realise it or not, in our own minds we have a vision or idea of what we're going to look like with grey hair. Biology has a horrible way of surprising even the most emotionally robust amongst us; **what we expect is often not what we get when it comes to grey hair** and a changing skin tone.

For example, you may have a preference for blonde shades and expect to get a shock of white hair, but your changing complexion and how your true grey hair colour reacts with bought hair colour, may make gentle brown undertones work best for you. Dealing with this unexpected outcome can be incredibly challenging emotionally.

For those of you who have been blonde all your lives, there is less emotional trauma and less work in gently transitioning to grey, or

PHOTO COURTESY: ZED PHOTOGRAPHY

silver or even white. Just a good style and cut is all that's necessary.

My advice is to think about the experience of colouring grey hair as an opportunity to radically (or subtly if you choose!) reinvent your look. Think of it as an adventure, or the beginning of a new chapter in your life, in which you can be free of anything that has held you back in the past.

At first, your adventure into this part of your reinvention, may shock you, and you may not like what you see in the mirror; that's because, for decades, you have seen yourself look a particular way. But as with everything, time smooths over the disappointment of not getting what you expected or hoped for. The first few compliments about your new hair colour from family and friends will help you learn to love it more!

5. *Treat Yourself To The Occasional Salon Visit*

Even if you're a dyed-in-the-wool home colour specialist, it's worth treating yourself with a **visit to a professional hairdresser once in a while.**

It's really very relaxing having someone massage your scalp, and it's an enjoyable way to pass time ... gossiping, flipping through magazines, and seeing what other people in the salon are wearing and having done with their hair.

An experienced hairdresser can **give you advice on new products to care for your hair,** and may have some

different ideas about colouring and styling for you. Pay close attention, and you can use their ideas when you get home.

As much as you can learn about new products from magazines and online reviews for colouring and caring for grey hair, it's only when a professional hairdresser touches your hair and assesses its texture and weight, that you get truly informed advice about what works for your hair. The cost of a hairdressing appointment can be worth it when you discover the **correct brand and strength of hair colour for your grey hair.**

An example of a completely natural look in colour and cut. The colour is similar to Anita's original hair colour but, because it isn't dark or overly vibrant, blends well with skin and eyes. Notice the blonde highlights, creating a natural feel. It's a good look.

PHOTO COURTESY: ANITA FURSLAND

IV. The Right Way To Bleach Grey Hair

It's not often seen as a positive, but one of the best things about **going grey** is that it **offers a blank palette**; a time to re-invent your look. You can do just about anything you want with it colour-wise, but as most colours contain bleach, when you want to return to grey, bleached hair can be a problem.

Bleaching grey hair, to become a platinum blonde or just to have your natural colour, **only** becomes a problem if you have continued to colour your hair after you have turned completely grey; while you're still pepper-and-salt, bleaching is not as tricky. At some point however, white or grey regrowth becomes too much to deal with, and as your skin tone changes and softens, it's easier to accept the inevitable.

The question is, how do you safely strip back dyed hair to the natural hair colour underneath, and what do you do with it when you get there?

Having A Plan To Go From A Dyed Dark Colour to Grey

The first thing to do is make a plan. The steps you need to take will depend on what you've done to your hair before now, and whether your hair is long or short.

Generally, the longer your hair the more consideration you'll need to give your approach ... especially if your goal is to strip out all of the colour. My recommendation is to consult a hairdresser if you're in this position.

Red pigments in hair dyes are the most difficult to get out of hair, so an attempt to jump straight from red, reddish-browns or mahogany to grey is the most difficult, which is why hairdressers will recommend against it. Instead they will want to work with you over a longer period (sometimes up to 2 years!), to give you the transition from colour to grey through selective tinting and bleaching over multiple appointments. This is not the hairdresser attempting to extort you, it is the practical reality of having a hair colour that is chemically challenging to get rid of, in such a way that you will still look fabulous during the transition.

If you have been dyeing your hair a dark colour, you'll also need to consider going through a few lighter colour changes before arriving at grey, rather than bleaching.

Bleaching to strip dark dyed hair colours back to the natural grey underneath is a notoriously unpredictable exercise. Women who have ventured to do this have many terrible stories to tell which, more often than not, end up with a long and very expensive visit to the hairdresser to cover the mess. It's not just a matter of getting an odd colour, there are risks to the scalp (burning the skin), the hair condition (hair falling out because it breaks off at the roots) and patchy results (colour stripping out unevenly).

If you're also trying to preserve beautiful long hair you'll want to be especially careful when deciding to bleach, because getting it wrong is far more noticeable when you have long locks.

If You Are More Than 30% Grey, Bleaching is Never A Good Idea

Bleach works by acting directly on the melanin (the body chemical that gives the hair its colour), inside the hair shaft. Because grey hair contains greatly reduced amounts of melanin, bleach will not always change the colour; instead, it will often just make the hair more brittle and dry; which you don't want.

As much as you might want to turn grey overnight by simply slapping on a ton of bleach, if more than 30% of your natural hair colour is grey, it's unlikely the ton of bleach will actually work at stripping out any colour.

Bleaching is a particularly harsh process no matter what condition your hair is in. When you're dealing with grey hair, it's even trickier.

If you're not sure how much grey you have underneath your dyed hair but are determined to get to grey quickly by bleaching, the best recommendation is to do a test first on a small piece of hair. Pick an area of your hair that is least exposed, where you would be comfortable having a silver streak if the bleaching works, and apply bleach to this section only. Make sure to bleach only in the concentrations and for the duration that the bleach instructions recommend. You will know if bleaching works for you or not, from the results you get using the prescribed concentration and leaving the bleach on for as long as recommended. Making the bleach stronger or leaving it on longer is only going to hurt you in a variety of different ways, destroying your hair or scalp.

When your test is successful, you can proceed small piece by small piece across the rest of your hair. It's not recommended to do your entire head in one go because hair reacts differently on different parts of your head. Things like exposure to sunlight, air conditioning, medications and pollution, all impact on your hair to make it react differently in different places. So take your time, plan a couple of quiet days and progressively bleach your hair, until you've got the final result you want. This will also give you a chance to allow some recovery time in between if you decide to re-bleach some pieces that haven't worked as you expected.

Bleaching Blonde To Grey

As already mentioned, **bleaching doesn't take your hair colour to grey if it's blonde**. Grey hair is already stripped of all colour, so bleach will have no impact on colour, just on condition.

In fact if you're blonde and wanting to get to grey, your best option is to stop colouring blonde all over and add streaks of blonde hair, gradually dyeing fewer streaks over time to reveal more of your natural grey each time. As counter-intuitive as this sounds, it's exactly the approach used by many women in the public eye.

When dyeing streaks into your grey hair, you'll want to ensure that you're using a product specifically formulated **for** grey hair; it will contain the additional chemicals needed to address the lack of melanin.

Fade To Grey Instead Of Bleaching To White

Hairdressers often recommend **using tints for best results in the transition** to grey hair, as good tints fade gradually and are gentler on the hair. The fade-as-you-grow option is also good for easing into white and silver hair because it reveals roots gradually, rather than leaving an obvious line of regrowth.

Using tints as an alternative to bleaching means that you can wear any hairstyle, and the condition of your hair is still manageable when it comes to styling. Whether you use a hair dryer, straighteners or curling wands, having hair that's in relatively good condition means you have more options when cutting and styling your grey hair... and as many women discover, grey hair has a very different texture and way of behaving than they are used to, so this can be enough of a challenge to deal with, without having hair in poor condition that's un-styleable as well; because of bleaching.

If however you're still determined to make the leap in one bound, one option that has **a good outcome is to cut your hair short**. This will really ensure that bleaching won't damage the overall look of longer hair, because it's now short! Your hair is able to recover more quickly if there is some damage (bleaching will only damage the exposed hair, not any new hair that grows through).

While a short cut can be a great option for a quick, dramatic change, the downside is that your hair has a much shorter breaking point and you'll find you need buckets of moisturising hair products and protective serums for heat styling until you are able to grow and cut off the bleached sections of your hair.

In addition, many women feel they are *giving in to old age,* **and being predictable**, by the act of cutting their hair short. Short hair seems to be redolent of aging gracefully and many women would rather age disgracefully; which seems a reasonable approach.

For many women the risks of bleaching are too great because they need to look great in public all the time, but in the end, it's up to you and your adventurous spirit as to whether you proceed with bleaching or not.

An example of the fabulous look achieved with blonde and dark highlights ... stunning.

V. Making The Transition From Dyed To Grey Hair

It's impossible to prepare yourself, when you are dyeing your hair to cover grey, for just how traumatic the change in your appearance may be when you decide to stop dyeing, and let the grey grow.

You may think that you'll be ready for an overnight change but few of us truly are; and let's be honest, it isn't an overnight change. All your life, you have seen yourself as a brunette, blonde, redhead or whatever colour it is you were, or chose to be. To suddenly be something that you've been conditioned to think of as old ... grey ... is often more of a psychological shock than you expect.

Slow and gradual change is more comfortable and easier to adjust to than a sudden and rapid change, which will make you respond violently.

With that in mind, when it comes to your hair colour, it's much easier for us to adjust to small changes than a dramatic overnight transition from coloured to grey hair. Remember, the darker your hair, the more drastic the change will appear, and the more you will need to reinvent your make-up to ensure you don't look too pale and washed-out, and to change your colours too!

Instead of making an overnight change from black to grey for example, which is never going to happen without destroying your hair, you can gently transition from black to brown to gentle steel to powerful silver. A process that requires patience and tenacity.

Let's Start With What Is Possible... Overnight Natural Grey Is Not

- There's no such thing as a magical grey hair dye. The idea that you can dye coloured hair with a grey colour and overnight look naturally grey haired is a myth.
- We've already talked about the risks of stripping the colour out of hair with bleach and it isn't a great option for grey hair which is more fragile than naturally pigmented hair.
- Lemon juice and sunlight is one of those old home remedies for naturally pigmented hair that has some lightening effects, though won't get you from coloured hair to grey no matter how much you'd like it to.
- You may have heard of the crushed vitamin C tablets approach to stripping dye colour out of hair; after more than 20 shampoos! (sounds suspiciously like your dye just fading to me).
- Then there are the formulations that basically are all designed to treat your hair so badly it can't hold the colour; any colour. For example, dandruff shampoo mixed with baking soda, clothes washing

powder or dishwashing liquid. None of which will work overnight, but will certainly ruin your hair overnight.

Once you've worked out the **im**possibilities, you arrive at the possibilities.

This was me, aged 58, with just a few highlights and a really boring hairstyle ... the grey in my hair was negligible at this stage.

Cutting Your Hair

Letting your hair grow out a little so that you can then cut it is the quickest way to grey hair. But do you **really** want to cut your hair?

This has been one of the most popular strategies over the last few years for those happy to have a regrowth stripe for a few weeks until the hair is long enough to cut.

It can be the most challenging strategy for your ego (and for your nerves!), because **you are changing both your cut and colour at the same time**. So if you've worn your hair long for many years, suddenly having a pixie cut and cold neck may be enough to make you completely break down when you get home from the hairdressers.

However, if you're happy to sport a scarf or hat, or a wig, or just smile through the initial growing period it **is** the quickest way to transition. Wear a scarf to keep your neck warm ...

Streaking Your Hair Colour

If you're after a gentler approach, highlights and low lights (foils ... blonde or dark) are the way to go. These will gently usher in strands of grey among the colour.

It's best to talk to your hairdresser about these, as getting the streaks to look natural needs skilled hands ... nobody wants to have a skunk stripe or look like a mangy cat. Nobody!

Coordinate with your hairdresser to get a time frame that is realistic so that appointments fit around important events where photographs are likely (weddings, birthdays and anniversaries come to mind).

The Courage to Transition

While going grey is far from the most traumatic experience in life, it's still a big change and can be very distressing; yet another challenge of the aging process to deal with.

Make sure you have support while you do it; men are often terrible at this, so round up your girlfriends, sisters, cousins and female confidantes to help you.

Although younger women (especially teenagers), won't necessarily understand the emotional impact of the change, they are fabulous for boosting your confidence with how your hair is looking. Friends are great for sharing the emotional journey and stories about their own experience, or those of others, which can help you feel more comfortable with the process. Family are often good for honest feedback, and may even give you the courage to consider other changes at the same time.

These days, with many influential women and young actresses embracing grey hair as a 'look', there's a 'coolness' factor around having grey hair. Flip through a few magazines or look at what's fashionable online.

Planning Your Transition

To make things even easier on yourself emotionally, **have a plan to make the transition over many months** (or years if necessary). This will give you time to adjust, for your hair to recover its natural strength, and for you to decide on a look that suits you … and while you're at it, consider an overall make-over to go with your new hair colour.

In my book *Hot Stuff: The Ultimate Guide to Style for Women of a Certain Age*, you'll find helpful information about fashion, colours, shapes and how to dress with style and flair when you're a woman of a certain age… if you're changing into a Silver-Haired Fox anyway, why not take it all the way.

An image of me at 62 with a strange hairstyle!

VI. Tips for Taming Wiry Grey Hair

Does wiry hair automatically mean a short haircut? Of course not. Longer, beautifully white hair, or sleek, stylish grey cuts can be some of the pleasures of life as you age. You just need to know how to tame that wibbly, wobbly, wiry grey hair.

Compared to your natural coloured hair, grey hair **is** wiry. It's unavoidable.

As individual hairs lose their pigment, they also lose some of the elements (including the cuticle) that protect them. The result is hair that is a little more porous, a little more brittle, and a little more likely to annoy anyone who is trying to create a good looking, sleek hairstyle; **sleek** being the operative word.

Removing The Frizz From Your Hair

There are two things to look at here: products that condition hair and products that eliminate frizz; all of which can be achieved with deep, deep conditioners and lightweight moisture-rich stylers combined with a flatiron. Believe it or not, you will need any/all of these to tame your wiry hair. You may even need to add another product to protect your hair from heat; hair dryer, curling tongs, straighteners and the like.

Conditioners are important, because they help protect the fragile hair and improve its general condition. Smother your hair in deep conditioner once a week and always leave a small amount (dime sized) of leave-in conditioner at the ends. Conditioner coats the cuticle itself, to make the hair look smoother; it is usually acidic which is why using **natural product conditioner like mayonnaise, lemon juice or vinegar**, works so well.

There are several ingredients to look for in a good conditioner ranging from natural oils to humectants to essential fatty acids, and there are almost as many types of conditioner as there are ingredients. Silicone in conditioner is something to be avoided unless you have dry, wiry hair and then it provides you with the slickness and smoothness you crave.

For frizz control products, silicone is a must.

Each hair shaft is made up of dead cells that have turned into keratin and binding material, together with small amounts of water. The dead cells overlap in layers, which form scales. The cuticle scales usually lie flat, **except** when your hair is grey and the cuticle scales stick out ... everywhere. Hence the reason for hair becoming frizzier with age. **Silicone smooths the scales down**, resulting in glossier, smoother hair.

Oil is still a good idea in a frizz control product, for extra conditioning power, but you may need to try a few products to find one that suits you. Going from frizz to oil slick is not what you want!

Lessons In Using Hair Products

Once you've got the right products on board, you need to know how to use them.

It starts with the way in which you wash your hair. You need to massage shampoo into your scalp and leave the ends of your hair as undisturbed as possible by stroking on the shampoo. Rinse thoroughly to remove the shampoo.

Smooth your conditioner on too, but starting from your scalp moving downwards right to the ends of your hair. Ideally you'll have more conditioner on the ends of your hair than on your scalp. This allows healthy new hair growth to receive a light conditioning and gives the conditioner time to work on the most exposed damaged ends.

When drying your hair, please don't do what so many people in the movies do and rub your hair into a frenzy of wispy knots. Instead, **wrap your hair in a towel** and allow it to absorb the moisture. After a few minutes take the towel off and find a dry part of the towel to re-wrap your hair and leave for another few moments. Finally take the towel off and pat the length of your hair between layers of towel to get it even drier. If your hair is short, you can towel it dry using a microfibre towel.

For styling, put your products on damp hair, and when you are styling with a blow dryer, use a rounded bristle brush and dry your hair completely, in small sections. The best way to dry your hair is not to dry it at all; allow it to air dry! Once your hair is dry, use your de-frizzing and any other products before using other styling tools as directed to ensure the heat doesn't damage your hair, like a straightening iron or curlers to finish.

While excessive styling can damage your hair, this kind of styling gets it all heading in the same direction and gives you control over how it all sits and looks.

Use a final light touch of hair spray to take care of those stubborn stray hairs and to keep everything in check, or just spritz the ends of your hair with an alcohol-free shine spray.

For those of us blessed with troublesome hair from the very beginning, this is just more of what we've been doing for years; but maybe with new products thrown in for good measure.

For the lucky few who have had the luxury of easy-to-style and manageable hair until now, all these new activities may seem excessive; all I can say is, give it a try and decide if you like the results.

Weathering The Weather

Sadly, now that you have a few wiry greys, you'll become like me (or your grandma was ... back in the day) ... obsessed with weather forecasts.

Your hair might be perfect as you open the door, but if it's a humid day you can go from sleek elf into fuzzy dandelion in a matter of seconds. Like it or not, **weather affects hair**. While you can put product in every day as a preventative, a far better answer is to pay attention to what the weather gods are throwing at you and style yourself accordingly.

That may mean extra **hair spray** if there's a lot of wind, a scarf if it is sunny and humid or lots of clips and accessories if it's cool and humid. For emergencies always have a few hair clips or pins stashed away in a pocket of your handbag or carry a chic scarf just in case you need to cover it all up.

If you've got the face for one, **hats can be your new best friend** on days when your hair just doesn't want to play ball. Of course, they are especially good to wear as the weather gets cooler; they stop the heat leaving your body and they protect your hair from the elements. In warmer weather, they hide a multitude of sins and stop you acquiring a sunburnt nose!

I can also recommend **a good wig** for those with a more adventurous spirit. They take a while to get the hang of but once you've had a compliment-filled-day-out wearing a wig, it's hard to resist the lure of trouble free hair a wig gives you. Raquel Welch has created a huge business from wigs, and she never has a bad hair day!

VII. 7 Silver-Haired Foxes Whose Hair Styles You May Want To Copy

It can be challenging to find pictures of women who proudly wear grey hair and look fabulous at the same time, when most magazines are filled with photos of young starlets who don't know of a world before mobile phones or lycra in everything. Although many of them now have had their hair dyed grey or silver. It has become very fashionable. Of course, it looks slightly different on a fresh and youthful face.

So I've put together a list of my personal favourite inspirational women who make being a woman of a certain age look effortless and attractive. You may have your own, and I hope you do, because these women are fantastic role models and we can absorb some of their wit and wisdom when it comes to looking fabulous as women over 50 and way beyond 50. They are forging a new way forward for us, and for future generations, and we should thank them.

For each of these lovely ladies we take a focused look at their hairstyle and figure out what it is that makes it work for them so that you can determine whether it would work for you.

There are lots of lessons to be learned by investigating the styling and fashion worn by women who find themselves constantly in front of an increasingly judgmental public eye.

7 Silver-Haired Foxes Who Look Fab with Grey Hair

Jamie Lee Curtis.

Curtis has been showing the world for years what it is to age with grace and power. While many women avoid short steel-grey hair, fearing it looks too masculine, Curtis is proof that it can work. Her secret is a blending of different tones. The cute pixie-cut that has set off her silver hair is a look that suits women with strong features who aren't afraid to show the world they are powerful and confident.

Dame Judi Dench.

Another star who has made short hair work is Dame Judi, and her hairstyle is a good contrast to Curtis' when you're looking for short style options. Dench's gently feathered cut is perfect for her gentle facial features, but it's the lighter colours which really make it work. It is a graceful yet feminine shorter style that many find easier to manage on a day to day basis.

Helen Mirren.

A woman who still makes young men sit up and blink, Mirren is skilled at making the most of her soft, silvery hair. There are two keys to her success: occasional blonde highlights, to help bring out a natural glow in her face, and obvious care that keeps her hair soft and manageable. It's not just her hairstyle that does the work though. Mirren pairs soft, feathery locks with bright lipsticks for a powerful impression.

Blythe Danner.

Blythe has always had quite thick hair, which she uses to her advantage these days for full-bodied, longer hairstyles. Although obviously grey, Danner accents her hair with blonde highlights for a vibrant look that still appears natural. She continues to wear a natural style of make-up in muted browns, earthy tones and pinks and maximises this look by wearing her hair in stranded waves with a side part.

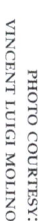

Meryl Streep.

Streep, whose natural hair colour is light brown, clung to her blonde look for many years, but has finally embraced the joys of silver – and what a change it makes. Her hair is thick and fine and Streep favours smooth, sleek silver looks, and usually offsets her hair with similarly sleek and stylish clothing; she is seldom seen in pastels. With finer hair, she favours pulled back styles with a sweeping fringe (or bangs) that either has a wave or some bounce in it for a bit of movement. She also favours a little wispiness around her face.

Dianne Keaton.

Keaton shows the way for anyone who doesn't have hours to spend on their hair. With a simple shoulder-length cut and brown low lights that set off her salt-and-pepper hair (of late she is moving heavily towards grey/silver - and it looks great!), Keaton manages and controls her locks with straightening. To give her hair a bit of shape around her face, a gentle flick is often added to the ends; it adds more life and accentuates the layer cut she prefers these days.

Carmen Dell'Orefice.

Carmen is the world's oldest working fashion model. At 86 she continues to grace the covers of magazines worldwide with her waves of silver white hair. She is an inspiration to us all and queen of the soft-wave-hairstyle that's swept away from the face. Carmen favours big hair in modern styles which allow her to wear darker make-up colours. Her coiffed looks are high maintenance, but worth it if you want to look this great.

You may feel it's impossible to match the high standards of these wonderful women when it comes to looking polished and fabulous, but I'm here to tell you ... it isn't. In 2008, I wrote a book called:

Hot Stuff: The Ultimate Guide to Style for Women of a Certain Age

with the aim of helping everyday women like myself regain their confidence so that they can step out in style every day of the year. As I researched and wrote this book, I found myself wondering at how such small adjustments to the things I was doing were able to transform the way I looked and in turn, how I felt about myself.

While I have no motivation to be a super model like Carmen Dell'Orefice (and I don't have the looks either), I now know that I can get really close to looking as fabulous as her if I want to - by simply paying more attention to the way I put on my make-up, choosing the right outfit and spending more time on my hair. I also know that with the information and helpful advice in this book, everyone can look and feel great every single day as well as on those special occasions.

VIII. Helping Your Grey Hair To Look Thicker And Fuller

Grey hair always creates a bit of a style conundrum. Its unique needs mean that styling can be a problem, particularly when a bit of bounce is wanted.

As hair thins, sleek and silky might be a look that's easier to maintain, but everyone needs a little voluptuousness once in a while. Luckily, there are ways to cheat it.

Your Weapons For Thick, Full Looking Hair

If you're after body that your hair doesn't have on its own, you need some weapons on standby. The most basic tools you'll need are a round brush and hair dryer. For truly luxurious silver hair, you'll need the heavy artillery of hair tongs, product, curlers and irons.

Start with a blow-dry. It's a simple way to give any hair more body. Use a round, bristled brush to pull out smallish sections of your hair and hold the blow-dryer several inches away from the hair.

This can be a particular help with greying hair, as it gets all of the strands, and more importantly, the scales of the cuticle, working together. By using a round brush, you're giving the hair a subtle curl, which translates into fuller hair when the job is done.

For a fuller look after the blow-drying is done, bend over and let your hair fall over your head, so that you're **drying with your head upside-down**. Drying this way puts gravity on your side although you will probably have to use tongs to settle the ends.

Products protect & style and it's a good idea to use styling products whenever blow-drying to protect the hair and help keep the body you put into it.

Styling products are essential for thicker, fuller hair, but make sure you look for **products that are designed to enhance volume** and won't weigh your hair down; if you don't know which are the best for you, ask the shop assistant or your hairdresser.

Generally, grey hair puts you at an advantage in the styling stakes because it takes on styles and absorbs product relatively easily, unless you're going through a phase where it's all just wiry and out of control. In which case, be prepared to put in a lot more time than you'd usually require for styling your hair, until your hair's condition settles down.

Handling Fine Hair

If you have fine silver hair, you'll need a little extra help. Look for hair products that are **designed for fine hair**, such as a root maximiser. This will help give you volume from your scalp rather than the body of your hair.

You may have thought you left them behind in the dark ages, but **curlers** have made a comeback and **are perfect for fine, silver hair**. Let's face it, there's nothing that can really beat heated curlers for a full head of glossy curls. Modern curler sets can create large, silky curls that can be worked into a naturally wavy hairstyle.

If you're someone who's short on time then grab a **curling wand** and see if that works for you. You won't have options on curl size as with heated rollers, but you will get your hair done quicker.

The secret to making the curls you create even more voluminous when styling is to pull each individual curl into five or six separated ones. The increased number of curls adds more volume instantly.

This is another image of me, this time aged 64. I have very fine, very thick hair which is a combination most hairdressers loathe. I still use heated rollers and when I travel I take a curling wand. If I don't, my hair looks like an explosion in a mattress factory.

You should avoid creams and gels when your hair is fine as they just weight it down and keep it close to your head. Instead use mousse and make sure you cover all strands so that they are both protected and given a coating that can be moulded.

A simple rule for everyday thicker, fuller hair is to use some volumising mousse and a simple blow-dry (head upside down!) which will get you good results.

What Your Hairdresser Does To Create Volume

Ask your hairdresser to cut the underneath layer of your hair slightly shorter than the top layer. This creates the illusion of fuller thicker hair; just make sure that your hairdresser uses scissors to cut the layers underneath and not a razor. A razor creates wispy frayed ends to your hair, and will give you frizz rather than volume. It's the blunt ends that scissors create that plump everything up.

Keeping the length of your hair well above shoulder length also creates an appearance of volume. As soon as your hair is sitting on the tops of your shoulders it loses visual impact giving it the illusion of appearing thinner.

Another trick used by hairdressers is to use coloured streaks; mixes of colour and shading create the illusion of density. Then when styling the hair they will allow it to get 80% dry on it's own before blow drying to get lift into hair. I'm sure you can remember a time when you were sitting in the chair with wet hair wondering when they were going to come back and finish it.

Hairdressers will also dry your hair with your parting in the wrong place and only at the end, when it's dry, do they flip the hair across to part it where you want, so that it is full from the roots out along your part. If they dried with your part in the right place from the start, your hair would sit flat to your head along the part.

Of course, if you have full hair in your crown but the body of your hair is thin, you can add volume with hair extensions. It's something young girls have taken to, that works wonders and you can too. And if you're open to the idea, there's always a wig.

IX. Make-up Tips For Looking Great With Grey Hair

There are a lot of people who react to grey hair with a cover-it-up- attitude; but more and more, women are embracing the change. If you've decided to go grey all the way and wear your silver locks with pride, you still have many decisions to make.

The way you accent your grey with make-up, rinses and clothing, can be the difference between **a rain cloud or a silver lining**.

The best news is that it's a great foundation for **bold colours**. Silver or grey hair is an excellent backdrop for a complete make-over in the make-up department, and because grey hair can make you look washed out, warmer tones in your make-up will make you look and feel brighter!

Start With The Basics

A luminescent moisturiser worn with a light foundation will make your face glow; or use a foundation that contains a luminescent moisturiser!

Personally, I'm not a fan of powder for women over 50, but if you are, use it sparingly ... too much and it can gather in your laughter lines! You'll look fine when you first apply the powder in some lights, but walk into a room with the wrong light, or go outside and look at yourself, or take a long hard look at the end of the day, and it's a very different face.

When applying foundation, don't forget your décolleté - neck and chest (unless you're wearing a high neck or polo neck), and because your chest is always darker than your face, match your foundation to your chest, not the inside of your wrist or the back of your hand. You want the colour to be uniform.

Adding A Fresh Glow

Add a little non-glitter blush; peachy pink or golden peach suit almost everybody once their hair is a lighter colour. A darker complexion can benefit from a deep candy-pink coloured blush. It's always a good idea, no matter what colour blush you are using, to do a quick check before you present yourself in public; use your camera phone to take a picture of yourself and see if you look natural or doll-like before stepping out. You don't want to go out looking like La Poupée!

Use blusher sparingly and only apply to the apples of your cheeks. This is not about face-shaping, it's about adding colour to brighten your complexion, so that it works against white, grey, and/or silver hair.

Helping Lips Look Luscious

As we age, our lips lose definition, and getting lip colour to stay where it's put can become tricky, so make sure you get into the habit of using a nude lip liner to provide your lips with a natural looking shape. In fact, wear nude colour liner all over your lips.

Once that's done, add some gloss and/or a lipstick a few shades darker than your own lips in rose, berry, peach, or apricot tones. The more natural the colour, the better it will look.

You may be tempted to use a vibrant colour like a "catwalk model" red so that your lips really pop. I'd never dissuade anyone from making a statement but I have to say, bright red lips often just don't cut it once you reach a certain age; your lips may become thinner and you may develop railroad tracks around your mouth (whether you have smoked or not!); rivulets along any fine lines around the mouth are an age giveaway, and really unattractive. But if this is important to you, put on a base layer, like a lipstick primer, to keep your colour in place as best you can.

Definition & Colour For Your Eyes

Avoid black kohl eyeliner and mascara, and smoky eye shadow … they generally don't work with grey hair. Try soft pencils around the eyes, in deep blues, greys or slate and blend well … you may have looked super sexy with a harsh line in your 20s or 30s but now it's time for something softer and different.

Try coloured mascara instead of black ... you may be an addict for a strong lash colour, but there is a point at which it no longer looks beautiful, as your skin tone and hair colour lightens. Mascara fans will also be horrified by my own personal rule which is to never put mascara on your bottom lashes once you have grey hair; it looks like little spider legs.

Eyebrows are the frame for your eyes, so if you have plucked them into oblivion, bring them back ... use a pencil in a soft brown or a dark gold/blonde, and always work from the outside towards the inner limit. Or you can use a tinted brow gel as a dye if your eyebrows are grey but still thick.

Getting New Ideas For Your Make-up

Take yourself into a department store and have your make-up done by someone in the cosmetics area. If you don't like the way it looks, go back and try a different brand on another day, and keep trying until you get a look that you like. It's important to remember that most of these girls are not professional make-up artistes! They happen to work for a cosmetic company and have been trained in the use of those cosmetics only ... they deliver a generic look ... and you are not generic. So be prepared to pay a few visits to get something that you like.

When you like what's been done, take a photograph of yourself with your mobile If you find no joy from the department store girls, you may consider going to a make-up class and learning the tips and tricks professional make-up artists use, and then applying the ideas they teach to your own lovely face.

In my book, Hot Stuff: The Ultimate Guide to Style for Women of a Certain Age, there is an entire chapter devoted to make-up which is entitled "**The Less is More Look**". It contains helpful tips and tricks on how to ensure your make-up looks natural and enhances your face, as well as some home truths about what doesn't work on mature skin - it will save you wasting money on cosmetics that just don't work for you.

Of course, you may have decided to wear your hair grey because you want to leave hairdressers and fuss behind. If that's the case, then consider doing the same with your face and just use a good, tinted moisturiser; women around the world have been doing this for a number of years, and now we have BB creams, you can too. Just make sure you don't look so pale that people start asking if you're ill ... use your phone again when you have moved to BB cream and are experimenting with a little lip gloss and something to highlight your eyes (you can have this look created for you in a store), so you have an image of the look you're going to re-create for yourself, and start wearing every day. This helps you replicate the look in the early stages while you're still mastering the new way to do your make-up.

X. Tips For Colouring Grey Eyebrows

The common rule for colouring eyebrows is a shade or two lighter - though fashion can sometime dictate something else. However, generally if you want to look natural, then the rule is one or two shades lighter than your hair colour.

When your hair turns grey however, things change. You may be looking to match your eyebrows to your grey hair, or trying to tweeze out the greys that clash with your hair colour, but either way, eyebrows can be a tricky area for dyeing.

Problems With Tinting Eyebrows

Tinting eyebrows can be difficult; because they are a defining feature on your face and are the frame for your eyes.

Your eyebrow hair is just as sensitive as hair on the head, meaning that it's prone to turning orange if bleached incorrectly, taking on too much colour if left too long, and even showing roots!

Eyebrows, like your hair, can thin as you get older, particularly if you've been plucking them for many years; as most women do. At the same time, the hair texture changes. For some women they will be coarser and for other women they become finer and wispier. Either development presents problems for tinting.

When the eyebrow hair is coarse, tinting becomes a balancing act between having the dye absorbed by the individual hairs and staining your skin or chemically burning it.

When eyebrow hair is fine, colour becomes a significant issue and there is the problem of hairs like these being more sensitive to chemicals.

If you're faced with either of these situations and become nervous about tinting your own eyebrows, better to seek professional assistance from either a hairdresser or beauty therapist/artist. They have the experience and the right dyes for making sure that your eyebrows are tinted correctly.

Follow The Steps To Get It Right

Eyebrows are dangerously near the eyes, so you must be extra careful when you dye.

Take your time to prepare everything correctly, especially the first time you dye your own eyebrows. Give yourself plenty of time, and to avoid embarrassment, don't attempt to dye just before you're supposed to be going out somewhere fancy. There's nothing worse that freshly dyed eyebrows that haven't been done properly because there wasn't enough time for the dye to take or for you to reduce the pigment stains on your skin. If you've had to scrub the skin around your eyebrows a little to remove staining, then swollen red eyebrows covered in makeup look very unattractive.

Putting a little Vaseline around the eye area protects the skin and prevents any horrible face-staining accidents. Again, take your time to apply the Vaseline properly, using a cotton bud (Q-tip), to reduce the amount of cover up or clean up you need to do after the dye is taken off.

The first thing to do is to use a product designed for grey eyebrow hair. It's tempting to just grab any old kit off the shelf, but remember that this is a delicate procedure. The home dye kits that aren't designed for greys often come out too dark, and some even wash out too easily meaning you've wasted your time which you will probably find really frustrating.

The colour you choose is important too. So try out a few different shades with make-up before you dye.

Eyebrow pencils and eyeshadow are very handy for testing out different colours and if your current make-up kit doesn't have a broad enough range pop down to your local chemist, drugstore or department store and try out a few testers.

You may be thinking at this point that I'm being overly cautious. I can assure you that even tinting your eyebrows the wrong colour just once will be enough to last a lifetime. There's a kind of horror moment when you see yourself in the mirror and think "there's no way I can go out looking like this!" or thoughts to that effect. So do the preparation and select the colour you think will best suit.

Once you decide on a shade that suits you, choose the right matching dye colour and stick to the minimum dyeing times recommended on the label. If you're uncertain when you get in front of a colour chart, ask someone else for their input or go for the lighter one that you feel is right.

They Won't Change Colour!

As frustrating as this can be, if the dye doesn't take the first few tries, try increasing the time you leave it on by small increments each time you dye. This all depends on your eyebrow hair.

Some hairdressers recommend using a little hair wax on the eyebrow to make sure the dye sticks, but it's up to you if you want or need to be this particular.

Finally, if you're in doubt, consult a hairdresser or beautician. It's a relatively small investment to make sure you don't walk around with shining black apostrophes lurking above your eyes!

Later you can work out what colour you need and do it at home yourself.

An Alternative

Have your eyebrows tattooed on. Before you take this step though, there are certain guidelines you must follow if you want the best result possible.

Find a really good make-up Permanent Makeup Artist (PMA). Your best bet is to talk to clients (and see them in the flesh!), who have used their services and are happy, or not, with the results. This is very, very important; you don't want a back yard butcher playing on your face.

Decide what you want and discuss it with the PMA at length. This is your face and it's essential you get exactly what you want.

Have different shapes and thicknesses, in different colours, pencilled on; take a photo of each alternative and decide which one works best. You are not trying to emulate the eyebrows you had when you were younger; you're trying to create something that is right for you now.

When you have decided which eyebrow you want, book the appointment.

Does it hurt? It isn't the most pleasant thing in the world but your PMA will put anaesthetic cream on the area about to be tattooed so, more than anything, it will just tickle!

If you have a fringe (bangs), you will want to wear it as low as possible for the first few days after the tattoo because your eyebrows, no matter the colour you have chosen, will be very dark. This is often the time when you will avoid going out, or feel it necessary to apologise to everybody. Don't worry - it **will** settle down!

This is probably the most lasting method of colouring your eyebrows, and you're not colouring the hair - just the skin. It will last for anything up 5 years.

Finally ...

At the risk of being boring, I just want to repeat what I said in the foreword; in case you didn't read it!

This is not a picture book; it's information on what is and what isn't possible to do with your grey hair, and how to do it.

The book answers the most often asked questions.

The images of me were taken over a 10 year period and illustrate the changes that you can go through during the transition phase. The most recent image of me is on the cover. I'm still not grey all over but am very pepper-and-salt. I have a mix of blonde and dark foils in my hair.

These illustrations of different hairstyles are taken from Hot Stuff.

A few useful websites for you to access if you are looking for more information:

About Melanin
www.bit.ly/1kQn4wx

About Melanocytes
www.1.usa.gov/1kOrxkE

About keratin
www.bit.ly/1nsuia9

The end of Grey Hair as we know it
https://en.wikipedia.org/wiki/Keratin#Clinical_significance

www.bit.ly/2lGbGu0

The amount the Average American woman spends
www.bit.ly/2miHtzG

The cost of hair dye
https://en.wikipedia.org/wiki/Hair_conditioner

Making grey hair look glam
http://dailym.ai/2mCmDu9

Smoking and premature greying
www.skintherapyletter.com/2010/15.6/2.html

Contact us if you want more tips and tricks:
Penelope Jane Whiteley

www.penelopewhiteley.com

pjw@penelopewhiteley.com

About Penelope Jane Whiteley

Penelope has become the Queen of Aging Disgracefully; she has been working with women over 50 for 20 years and is always thrilled when she helps another woman complete her metamorphosis and become the woman she was always meant to be. A mentor and coach, a writer and speaker, a stylist and a designer, she is able to offer women a complete change in Attitude and a Metamorphosis which will take them from Chrysalis to Butterfly.